The **100** Days
of "I Am"
Affirmations

Suzi Sung

About The Author

This is Suzi Sung's third book in the "100 Days" series and while she still isn't an internationally renowned author, or a New York Times Best Seller, nothing has stopped her from writing book after book.

Instead of climbing Mount Everest, she's decided that climbing out of a dark hole of low self-esteem, and helping others do the same, is an equally worthy accomplishment. She has no interest in pursuing a degree – the only pieces of paper that matter to her are the ones she writes her affirmations and goals on.

She knows that in order for an affirmation to work, you can't just say it – you need to feel it and believe it.

Which is why she wrote this book for you.

Contents

Introduction

The words we say to ourselves are important because we become what we think and feel. Start your day right with the affirmation journal, change your negative self-talk and begin to see the changes to your life..

Affirm it- Say your affirmation out loud and repeat it throughout the day.

Feel it-Read the words and begin to feel that you are your affirmation.

Believe it-Write down why you are your affirmation and see the proof.

SELF-WORTH AFFIRMATIONS

I
Am
Good Enough

Regardless of how you feel.
Or what anyone else has said to you.
No matter what anyone else thinks about you.
Regardless of what is going on in your life right now.
Don't ever forget that you are good enough just as you are.

I am good enough because

I CAN DO ANYTHING I PUT

MY MIND TO

I am good enough because

I am good enough because

I
Am
Worthy

You can have anything.
You can live the life you want.
You can have the love you want.
You can have the career you want.
You can have the experiences you want.
You can have it all because you are worthy right now.

I am worthy because

....
....
....

I am worthy because

....
....
....

I am worthy because

....
....
....

I
Am
Deserving

You deserve to have what you want in life.
What you already have, you deserve.
Everything you desire is yours.
You deserve happiness.
You deserve freedom.
You deserve love.
You deserve
it all.

I am deserving because

....

....

....

I am deserving because

....

....

....

I am deserving because

....

....

....

I
Am
Strong

You are strong.
Strength lies within all of us.
Even though you may not feel like it at times.
Even though you may have had moments of weakness.
Remember that your strength is always with you.
Believe you can handle anything.
Believe you can do anything.
Believe you are strong.

I am strong because

I CAN DO iT BY MYSELF

I am strong because

I am strong because

I
Am
Courageous

Your fears don't define you.
Your fears don't control you.
You can overcome your fears.
Your fears can't hold you back.
When you choose courage over fear,
You have the power to change your life.

I am courageous because

I ALWAYS TAKE THE LEAP
AS FAST AS I CAN

I am courageous because

i FACE AND FiGHT MY
BATTLES

I am courageous because

I
Am
Amazing

No one can be you.
No one can do what you do.
You were born to be amazing.
You are who you're supposed to be.
There is greatness in every single person.
So remember that you are already amazing.

I am amazing because

....

....

....

I am amazing because

....

....

....

I am amazing because

....

....

....

I
Am
Loved

You can have the love you want.
You deserve to be loved.
Love is all around you.
Believe in love.
You are loved.

I am loved because

....

....

....

I am loved because

....

....

....

I am loved because

....

....

....

I
Am
Forgiving

Free yourself with forgiveness.
Forgive yourself for what has passed.
Choose to forgive those who have wronged you.
Not because they deserve it, but because you do.
Let go of the hurt and anger; allow healing to take its place.

I am forgiving because

....
....
....

I am forgiving because

....
....
....

I am forgiving because

....
....
....

I
Am
Calm

When your calmness has been interrupted, become aware.
Accept that the feelings of anxiousness and anger are present.
Consciously choose to release these feelings and find your way back to calm.
Take deep invigorating breaths in and breathe out all the negativity.
Let the relaxation take over and feel calmness wash over you.

I am calm because

....
....
....

I am calm because

....
....
....

I am calm because

....
....
....

I
Am
Respected

You deserve respect.
You are in control of how you are treated.
You don't have to allow disrespectful situations into your life.
You can choose to remove yourself from those who cannot show you respect.
When you believe and act like you are worthy of respect, you will be respected.

I am respected because

....
....
....

I am respected because

....
....
....

I am respected because

....
....
....

I
Am
Powerful

You are so powerful.
Your power lies within you.
You are in control of your power.
You can take your power back anytime.
You have the power to do anything you want.
You are capable of anything because you are powerful.

I am powerful because

....
....
....

I am powerful because

....
....
....

I am powerful because

....
....
....

I
Am
Confident

Confidence is all in the mind.
Breathe in confidence and breathe out self doubt.
When you feel good, your confidence will shine through.
Feel confident in the things you do and the decisions you make.
When you have confidence, you can do anything you set your mind to.

I am confident because

....

....

....

I am confident because

....

....

....

I am confident because

....

....

....

I
Am
Beautiful

Beauty can be found in everything.
It does not come from what you wear.
It does not come from what you look like.
It does not come from what your dress size is.
Your beauty is unique and it comes from within..
Always remember that you are beautiful just as you are.

I am beautiful because

....

....

....

I am beautiful because

....

....

....

I am beautiful because

....

....

....

I
Am
Fearless

Fear exists only in the mind.
False Evidence Appearing Real.
Do the thing that scares you the most.
You'll see there was nothing to be afraid of.
You either control your fear or it controls you.
Face your fears and watch them fade away.
You are fearless.

I am fearless because

....

....

....

I am fearless because

....

....

....

I am fearless because

....

....

....

I
Am
A Badass

You can handle anyone.
You can handle anything.
You can ask for what you want.
You can dismiss what you don't want.
You can show everyone how amazing you are.
You can do all of this because you are a badass.

I am a badass because

....

....

....

I am a badass because

....

....

....

I am a badass because

....

....

....

I
Am
Playful

Feel light and carefree.
Let go of worry and stress.
Find a way to make your day fun.
Play is not just for children.
You can be playful too.

I am playful because

....
....
....

I am playful because

....
....
....

I am playful because

....
....
....

I
Am
Honest

When you choose honesty over pleasing everyone, you attract honest people.
Decide that you will not make a place for lies in your life.
Leave the lies for the liars and deception for the deceitful.
Let honesty and integrity be who you are.
Be honest with yourself and others.
The truth will set you free.

I am honest because

....
....
....

I am honest because

....
....
....

I am honest because

....
....
....

I
Am
Accepting Myself

Forget about the people who choose not to accept who you are right now.
They cannot take your power when you don't let their words hurt you.
Stop judging yourself because who you are today is enough.
When you accept who you are that's all that matters.
When you feel acceptance from within you,
You attract more of it to you.

I am accepting myself because

....
....
....

I am accepting myself because

....
....
....

I am accepting myself because

....
....
....

I
Am
Irreplaceable

There is only one you.
No one else can be you.
No one else can replace you.
You are irreplaceable in every way.
Remember how amazing you really are.

I am irreplaceable because

....
....
....

I am irreplaceable because

....
....
....

I am irreplaceable because

....
....
....

I
Am
Setting Boundaries

You can say no when you need to.
You can say yes when you want to.
You do not need to please everyone.
You can ask for your needs to be met.
You can walk away when they are not met.
You can set your boundaries however you want to..

I am setting boundaries because

....
....
....

I am setting boundaries because

....
....
....

I am setting boundaries because

....
....
....

I
Am
Raising My Standards

Your standards dictate your circumstances.
You deserve to have people in your life that put in what you do.
Your standards will be met by people who are worthy of being around you.
Stand by your standards and refuse anyone who cannot match your standards.
Raise your standards; it comes down to who you give your time to and how you are treated.

I am raising my standards because

....
....
....

I am raising my standards because

....
....
....

I am raising my standards because

....
....
....

I
Am
Saying No

Do what makes you happy.
You don't need to please everyone.
You can say no to what doesn't serve you.
You can say no to anyone who treats you badly.
You can say no to any situation that brings you down.
You can say no to your friends and family without feeling guilty.
Say no to the things that don't work for you and only say yes to what does.

I am saying no to

....
....
....

I am saying no to

....
....
....

I am saying no to

....
....
....

I
Am
Balanced

You can be kind and still set good boundaries for yourself.
You can be strong and still show vulnerability to others.
You can be sweet and still have a badass side of you.
You can be motivated and still have lazy days.
You can be both; you don't have to choose.
It's about choosing the right time.
It's about finding balance.

I am balanced because

....

....

....

I am balanced because

....

....

....

I am balanced because

....

....

....

I
Am
Brave

You can handle anything.
You can overcome anything.
You can face your fears and win.
You can do anything you put your mind to.
Be brave, take risks, and let amazing things happen.

I am brave because

....

....

....

I am brave because

....

....

....

I am brave because

....

....

....

I
Am
Intelligent

Your intelligence is not determined by your education.
Intelligence comes in so many different ways.
You can be smart just by choosing to be.
You can choose to learn more.
You can choose to adapt.
You can be smart
without a
degree.

I am smart because

....

....

....

I am smart because

....

....

....

I am smart because

....

....

....

I
Am
Special

You are meant for more.
You were born to do great things.
You can have the life of your dreams.
You are destined for a life of joy and happiness.
You can have anything you want, because you are special

I am special because

....

....

....

I am special because

....

....

....

I am special because

....

....

....

I
Am
Valued

You are important.
Your needs are important.
Who you are right now is enough.
Your value is not based on your success.
You can still bring value to other people's lives.
You are valued and you matter more than you will ever know.

I am valued because

....
....
....

I am valued because

....
....
....

I am valued because

....
....
....

WEALTH AFFIRMATIONS

I
Am
A Money Magnet

Money is everywhere; there is more than enough.
Money is just energy, like everything else.
Money is always flowing towards you.
You can have all the money you want.
It wants to come to you.
Believe it; claim it.

I am a money magnet because

....
....
....

I am a money magnet because

....
....
....

I am a money magnet because

....
....
....

I
Am
Attracting Wealth

You can attract wealth easily and quickly.
Believe it and believe you deserve it.
You are surrounded by wealth.
It is always flowing to you.
It wants to be with you.
Let it flow to you.
Claim it.

I am attracting wealth because

....
....
....

I am attracting wealth because

....
....
....

I am attracting wealth because

....
....
....

I
Am
Rich

Align with richness and begin to see riches everywhere.
Wealth and riches are always flowing towards you.
Every day, you are becoming richer and richer.
You will always have more than enough.
Riches come easily and effortlessly.
Richness surrounds you.

I am rich because

....

....

....

I am rich because

....

....

....

I am rich because

....

....

....

I
Am
Receiving
Money Easily

Money surrounds you.
Money is everywhere you look.
Money always finds its way to you.
You can have all the money you want.
Money loves you and wants to be with you.

I am receiving money easily because

....
....
....

I am receiving money easily because

....
....
....

I am receiving money easily because

....
....
....

I
Am
Deserving of Money

You are worthy of the money you want.
You can have the money you want.
Allow money to come to you.
Believe you can have it.
You deserve money.
It will find you.
Trust it will.

I am deserving of money because

....
....
....

I am deserving of money because

....
....
....

I am deserving of money because

....
....
....

I
Am
Financially Abundant

What you believe about money becomes true for you.
There is more than enough money for everyone.
Money is energy and energy is abundant.
Money is constantly flowing.
Money is everywhere.
Money is yours.

I am financially abundant because

....
....
....

I am financially abundant because

....
....
....

I am financially abundant because

....
....
....

I
Am
Generous

Give generously.
Give without fear of lack.
Whatever you give out, you get back.
Give to those, even when they cannot give back.
When you are generous, you live a life of abundance.

I am generous because

....
....
....

I am generous because

....
....
....

I am generous because

....
....
....

I
Am
Financially Free

Money is everywhere.
Be open to money energy.
You have more than enough.
You have all the money you need.
You are free to do whatever you want.
Money always appears when you need it.
You will always find the money to do what you want.

I am financially free because

....
....
....

I am financially free because

....
....
....

I am financially free because

....
....
....

I
Am
Creating Multiple
Streams of Income

You can have multiple sources of income.
Your job is not the only way to make money.
There are opportunities to make money everywhere.
If you want to make more money, you can—just by choosing to.
When you look for several streams of income, they will find you too.
You are wealthy in many ways; when you choose to believe it, you
will see it.

I am wealthy in many ways because

....

....

....

I am wealthy in many ways because

....

....

....

I am wealthy in many ways because

....

....

....

HEALTH
AFFIRMATIONS

I
Am
Taking Care of Me

Feed your body with nutrients.
Feed your skin with nourishment.
Feed your mind with positive thoughts.
Feed your soul with love and forgiveness.
Do what feels good and right for you right now.
Take care of every single part of you; you deserve it.

I am taking care of me because

....

....

....

I am taking care of me because

....

....

....

I am taking care of me because

....

....

....

I
Am
Healthy

A healthy body will feel good.
A healthy mind can handle anything.
Healthy, vibrant energy flows through your body.
Choose to nourish your mind and body with goodness.
Choose to attract wellbeing to your mind, body, and soul.
Welcome healthy and positive energy to flow through you.

I am healthy because

....
....
....

I am healthy because

....
....
....

I am healthy because

....
....
....

I
Am
Energised

Repeat this over and over and feel the energy rush through your body.

Feel yourself spring to life with each breath you take and feel invigorated.

Picture yourself radiating this energy and putting it into everything you do.

Imagine yourself being full of vitality and see your day ahead as lively and vibrant.

Everything you do today will be full of life and excitement because you are energised.

I am energised because

....

....

....

I am energised because

....

....

....

I am energised because

....

....

....

I
Am
Relaxed

Take a deep breath in and breathe out slowly.
Feel the anxiety and tension leave as you breathe out.
Feel your shoulders drop and a wave of relaxation wash over.
Allow your mind to be clear of any unwanted thoughts and focus on your breath.
Breathe in and out, in and out, until you feel completely relaxed and free from stress.

I am relaxed because

....
....
....

I am relaxed because

....
....
....

I am relaxed because

....
....
....

I
Am
Radiant

Feel love radiate through you.
Feel happiness radiate through you.
Feel confidence radiate through you.
Feel appreciation radiate through you.
Imagine a bright light shining through you.
Your radiance is glowing with positive energy.
Send it out to the universe and it will return light to you.

I am radiant because

....
....
....

I am radiant because

....
....
....

I am radiant because

....
....
....

I
Am
Healing

You can heal yourself.
Your mind can heal itself.
Your body can heal itself.
You can heal from heartbreak.
You can heal from disappointment.
You can heal your childhood wounds.
You have the power within you to heal.
You are healing your mind, body, and soul.

I am healing because

....
....
....

I am healing because

....
....
....

I am healing because

....
....
....

MOTIVATION
AFFIRMATIONS

I
Am
Ready

Are you ready for the day ahead?
Are you ready to achieve your goals?
Are you ready to take on the world?
Are you ready to see the good in your day?
Are you ready to be the person you want to be?
Are you ready for any challenges you may face?
Of course you are, because you were born ready!

I am ready because

....
....
....

I am ready because

....
....
....

I am ready because

....
....
....

I
Am
Capable

You can be anyone you want.
You can do anything you want.
You can have anything you want.
You can have it all because you are capable.

I am capable because

....

....

....

I am capable because

....

....

....

I am capable because

....

....

....

I
Am
Motivated

You can do this.
Motivation is a choice.
Choose to work on your goals.
Let go of your excuses and just go for it.
Forgive yourself for the days when you didn't do much.
Remember that every day is another day to change your life.
Visualise your goal; feel the motivation flow through you and make a start.

I am motivated because

....

....

....

I am motivated because

....

....

....

I am motivated because

....

....

....

I
Am
Inspired

Inspiration is everywhere.
Inspiration will always find you.
When you let go, that's when you see it.
Let inspiration come to you in its own time.
Relax and allow yourself to be in the moment.
Release resistance to the outcome and let inspiration in.

I am inspired because

....
....
....

I am inspired because

....
....
....

I am inspired because

....
....
....

I
Am
Successful

Success is for anyone willing to work for it.
The key to success is consistency.
Success is a state of mind.
You can be successful.
You deserve it.

I am successful because

....
....
....

I am successful because

....
....
....

I am successful because

....
....
....

I
Am
Already Doing
My Best Today

Forget about what everyone else is doing.
It doesn't matter how far ahead they are.
You don't have to compare yourself.
You are already doing your best.
Whatever your best looks like.
It is already enough.

I am doing my best today because

....

....

....

I am doing my best today because

....

....

....

I am doing my best today because

....

....

....

I
Am
Becoming
Better Every Day

Every day is a new experience.
Every day is another day to grow.
Every day teaches you a new lesson.
Every day is another chance to be better.
Every day you are becoming a new version of you.

I am becoming better every day because

....
....
....

I am becoming better every day because

....
....
....

I am becoming better every day because

....
....
....

I
Am
Stepping Out of My
Comfort Zone

Change can only happen outside of the comfort zone.
It may feel safe but nothing ever changes here.
Nothing in your life can grow in this zone.
Face your fears and step outside.
Choose growth over comfort.

I am stepping out of my comfort zone because

....

....

....

I am stepping out of my comfort zone because

....

....

....

I am stepping out of my comfort zone because

....

....

....

I
Am
Making Time

We all have 24hrs in a day.
Make your goals your priority.
"I don't have time" is just an excuse.
It only distracts you from what you want.
How you spend your time affects your outcome.
You can make time for anything when you choose to.
Make time right now and start to make great things happen.

I am making time because

....
....
....

I am making time because

....
....
....

I am making time because

....
....
....

I
Am
Doing Enough

Wherever you are, you are in the right place.
Whatever your best looks like is enough.
Let go of guilt and negative self-talk.
You are already amazing.
You are good enough.

I am doing enough because

....

....

....

I am doing enough because

....

....

....

I am doing enough because

....

....

....

I
Am
Proud of Myself

Whatever you have gone through.
However far you have come.
Whoever you have become.
Feel proud to be you.

I am proud of myself because

....
....
....

I am proud of myself because

....
....
....

I am proud of myself because

....
....
....

I
Am
Focussed

Stay focussed on what you want, not what you don't want.
Keep your goal at the forefront of your mind.
Keep moving forward and don't give up.
Visualise your dreams coming true.
Stay focussed, you will get there.

I am focussed because

....
....
....

I am focussed because

....
....
....

I am focussed because

....
....
....

I
Am
In Control

You are the creator of your life.
You can choose how you live it.
You can decide what you want.
You can take back your power.
You are in control of you.

I am in control because

....
....
....

I am in control because

....
....
....

I am in control because

....
....
....

I
Am
A Fighter

People only fail when they give up; keep going.
You are stronger than you think; you can do this.
Show the world what you are made of; you've got this.
When you fall down, get back up and fight for what you want.

I am a fighter because

....
....
....

I am a fighter because

....
....
....

I am a fighter because

....
....
....

I
Am
Capable of Greatness

Everything you need to be great, you already have.
Your belief affects what you will choose to do.
But there is nothing you cannot do.
Greatness is in all of us.
You are already great.
You can do anything.

I am capable of greatness because

of the person i am

I am capable of greatness because

I am capable of greatness because

I
Am
Already Doing It

Whenever you are worried about achieving your goals.
Whenever you worry about living your life the way you want.
Whenever you feel like you are not the person that you want to be.
Whenever you feel like you're not doing enough work to get to where you want.
Whenever you tell yourself how much you need to do, remember that you are already doing it.
Right now, in this moment, you are doing everything you need to; if you are not, you can start now.

I am already doing it because

....
....
....

I am already doing it because

....
....
....

I am already doing it because

....
....
....

I
Am
Changing My Life

Every second of every minute of every hour is a chance to make a change.
Whatever you do today will affect your life tomorrow.
Take every moment to make a difference.
Choose to live the life of your dreams.
Choose to change your life.

I am changing my life because

....
....
....

I am changing my life because

....
....
....

I am changing my life because

....
....
....

I
Am
Resourceful

Whenever you are stuck, you will find a way out.
Whenever you feel lost, you will find your way back.
Whenever you hit a brick wall, you will find a way to break it.
Whenever you are faced with a problem, you will find a solution.
Whenever you come across challenges, you will find a way around them.
You can and will overcome anything that stands in your way because you are resourceful.

I am resourceful because

....

....

....

I am resourceful because

....

....

....

I am resourceful because

....

....

....

I
Am
Making
Decisions Easily

You cannot make a wrong choice.
Everything you do, you can learn from.
Even if a decision was bad, it was necessary.
Don't let fear of what may happen make you indecisive.
Trust that the choices you make will always work for you.
Every decision you make is a step closer to where you want to be.
Making a decision, whether good or bad, is better than making no decision at all.

I am making decisions easily because

....
....
....

I am making decisions easily because

....
....
....

I am making decisions easily because

....
....
....

I
Am
Acknowledging
My Excuses

Excuses come from the ego and mask themselves as valid reasons.
Whatever your excuse is, it comes from a place of fear.
Excuses try to keep you in your comfort zone.
Find out which excuses are stopping you.
Recognise them and admit to them.
Acknowledge your excuses.
Stop making them.

I am acknowledging my excuses because

....

....

....

I am acknowledging my excuses because

....

....

....

I am acknowledging my excuses because

....

....

....

I
Am
Limitless

The only limits you have are the ones that you created.
Whatever you think is your best, will be your best.
You can remove the ceiling above you.
Believe your abilities are endless.
Believe anything is possible.
Believe you are
limitless.

I am limitless because

....

....

....

I am limitless because

....

....

....

I am limitless because

....

....

....

MINDFULNESS
AFFIRMATIONS

I
Am
Kind

A small act of kindness can make a big difference to someone's day.
Try to be kind to everyone that crosses your path today.
Choose to make kindness a part of who you are.
Being kind to others is very important.
But so is being kind to yourself.

I am kind because

....
....
....

I am kind because

....
....
....

I am kind because

....
....
....

I
Am
Grateful

There is always something to be grateful about.
Find something you are grateful for today.
Feel the gratitude fill up your heart.
Let it stay with you all day.
Be grateful.

I am grateful because

....

....

....

I am grateful because

....

....

....

I am grateful because

....

....

....

I
Am
Free

You are free to be who you want.
You are free to do what you want.
You are free to have what you want.
Choose to be free and you will be free.

I am free because

....
....
....

I am free because

....
....
....

I am free because

....
....
....

I
Am
Compassionate

Be kind to yourself.
Be present in every moment.
Compassion starts from within.
Listen carefully to your thoughts.
Release judgment towards yourself.
Learn to be compassionate towards yourself.
When you do, you will become compassionate towards others.

I am compassionate because

....

....

....

I am compassionate because

....

....

....

I am compassionate because

....

....

....

I
Am
Making Progress

Every day is a chance to grow.
Every setback is teaching you.
Every experience is shaping you.
Every joyful moment is rewarding you.
Everything that is happening is changing you.
Every day you are making progress towards your goals.

I am making progress because

....

....

....

I am making progress because

....

....

....

I am making progress because

....

....

....

I
Am
Being Patient

Trust that everything is coming to you at the right time.
Everything is coming to you in the right way.
Impatience only adds resistance.
Let go of the outcome.
Have patience.
It will come.

I am being patient because

....
....
....

I am being patient because

....
....
....

I am being patient because

....
....
....

I
Am
Evolving

Who you are today is not who you were yesterday.
Who you'll be tomorrow will not be who you are today.
Focus on this present moment and on who you are right now.
Forgive who you were in the past and remember you are always evolving.

I am evolving because

....
....
....

I am evolving because

....
....
....

I am evolving because

....
....
....

I
Am
Going with the Flow

Let go and surrender to the flow of your life.
Know that everything is always happening for you.
Trust that the answers will show themselves in time.
Release resistance to the things that cannot be changed.
Let your situation unfold and the reasons for it reveal itself.
Go with the flow of life and let it take you where you're meant to be.

I am going with the flow because

. . . .

. . . .

. . . .

I am going with the flow because

. . . .

. . . .

. . . .

I am going with the flow because

. . . .

. . . .

. . . .

I
Am
Allowing Change

Change allows growth.
Change allows for newness.
Change allows for excitement.
Change allows for understanding.
Change can set you free if you let it.
Learn to accept change and release resistance.
Allow change to happen and see amazing things happen.

I am allowing change because

....

....

....

I am allowing change because

....

....

....

I am allowing change because

....

....

....

I
Am
Open to New
Opportunities

New opportunities are everywhere.
When something new comes along, let it in.
Step out of your comfort zone and into the unfamiliar.
Opportunities become visible when you allow yourself to see them.
Be open to new ideas and other options; when you are stuck, they will set you free.

I am open to new opportunities because

....
....
....

I am open to new opportunities because

....
....
....

I am open to new opportunities because

....
....
....

I
Am
Letting Go

The fears that keep you stuck, you will conquer.
The weights that hold you down have been removed.
Your focus on the outcome has been redirected to the present.
The memories of the past that hold you back have been released.
Anything that was stopping you from moving forward has been dealt with.
You have let go of what no longer serves you; believe it, feel it, and release it.

I am letting go because

....
....
....

I am letting go because

....
....
....

I am letting go because

....
....
....

I
Am
Adapting to Change

Welcome change that is unpreventable.
Release resistance and let go of what cannot be.
Be flexible when it comes to situations you can't control.
Allow yourself to become adaptable and make your life easier.
You can adapt to change easier when you choose to accept and allow it.

I am adapting to change because

....
....
....

I am adapting to change because

....
....
....

I am adapting to change because

....
....
....

I
Am
Moving On

*You can walk away from relationships, jobs, and people that no
longer work for you.*
You can choose to step out of situations that no longer bring you joy.
Move away from the past and do what makes you happy today.
Close the chapter in your life that you want to be done with.
Choose to move on from anything that brings you down.
Take back control of your life and let go of the past.

I am moving on because

....
....
....

I am moving on because

....
....
....

I am moving on because

....
....
....

I
Am
Understanding

Choose to be more understanding of situations you're not used to.
Choose to be more understanding of things you don't agree with.
Choose to be more understanding of actions you wouldn't take.
Choose to be understanding of people who differ from you.
Choose to be more understanding to yourself and others.
When you are understanding, you appreciate more.

I am understanding because

....

....

....

I am understanding because

....

....

....

I am understanding because

....

....

....

I
Am
Removing Obstacles

The things that stand in your way will not always be there.
You can overcome any obstacles that get in your road.
Anything that was blocking you will fade away.
Choose to remove obstacles and you will.
You will defeat the challenges you face.

I am removing obstacles because

....

....

....

I am removing obstacles because

....

....

....

I am removing obstacles because

....

....

....

I
Am
Removing Judgment

Let go of the judgment of people's actions.
Don't allow others' judgment of you, affect you.
You are not in their shoes and they are not in yours.
Realize that judgment is based on opinion and not fact.
Remove judgment on yourself, on others, and release it from your
life.

I am removing judgment because

....
....
....

I am removing judgment because

....
....
....

I am removing judgment because

....
....
....

I
Am
Open-Minded

There is choice in everything we do.
You can choose to see more than one option.
You can choose to understand another point of view.
You can choose to welcome new experiences and people.
You can choose to be open-minded and give yourself more choices
in life.

I am open-minded because

....
....
....

I am open-minded because

....
....
....

I am open-minded because

....
....
....

I
Am
Humble

Lack cannot exist in a state of humbleness.
Realize what you already have and feel grateful.
You can love what you have right now and still aim for more.
Feel how lucky you are to be you and know that you are blessed.
When you are humble with your words and your actions; you have enough.

I am humble because

....

....

....

I am humble because

....

....

....

I am humble because

....

....

....

I
Am
Choosing to
See the Good

Choose to find the good in everything that happens today.
Look for the positives in any situation you come upon.
Look for the good in the people you come across.
Look for the good in the things that you do.
Choose to see good all day, every day.
And it will show itself to you.

I am choosing to see the good because

....
....
....

I am choosing to see the good because

....
....
....

I am choosing to see the good because

....
....
....

I
Am
Saying Yes

When you say yes, you say that you are open to receiving.
Say yes because unplanned nights are the best nights.
Say yes to opportunities even if they scare you.
Say yes, even if you think you can't do it.
Say yes because anything can happen.

I am saying yes to

....

....

....

I am saying yes to

....

....

....

I am saying yes to

....

....

....

I
Am
Positive

Look for the positives in any situation and strengthen your mindset.
Choose to be more positive and notice how your experiences change.
When you start to focus more on the good, you get more good.
You can find a positive in anything, you just have to look.
Rid yourself of negativity and see your life light up.
Radiate positive energy and feel it enlighten you.

I am positive because

....
....
....

I am positive because

....
....
....

I am positive because

....
....
....

I
Am
Becoming the Best
Version of Me

Choose to be your best self every day.
Choose to learn something new every day.
Choose to become more self-aware every day.
Choose to do the things that make you better every day.
Choose to break away from the old you that is no longer you.
Choose to become the best version of yourself every day and change
your life.

I am becoming the best version of me because

....

....

....

I am becoming the best version of me because

....

....

....

I am becoming the best version of me because

....

....

....

I
Am
Happy

Happiness is possible.
Allow yourself to be happy.
Believe that you can be happy.
Know that you deserve to be happy.
Find little things that make you happy every day.
The happier you are in the present, the happier you'll be in the future.

I am happy because

....
....
....

I am happy because

....
....
....

I am happy because

....
....
....

SPIRITUAL AFFIRMATIONS

I
Am
Divinely Guided

Your heart is always guiding you.
Your angels are always guiding you.
Your intuition is always guiding you.
Divine guidance is always working for you.
Even when it doesn't feel like it, it's protecting you.
Learn to see the signs and be divinely guided to joy.

I am divinely guided because

....

....

....

I am divinely guided because

....

....

....

I am divinely guided because

....

....

....

I
Am
Present

Breathe in and out forfour, feel your chest rise and fall.
Close your eyes and focus on your breath.
The past and future do not matter.
Picture where you are right now.
All you have is this moment.
You are present.

I am present because

....
....
....

I am present because

....
....
....

I am present because

....
....
....

I
Am
Protected

You are protected.
Angels are looking after you.
Your intuition will always protect you.
Sometimes bad things will happen to you because
You are being protected from worse things happening to you.

I am protected because

....
....
....

I am protected because

....
....
....

I am protected because

....
....
....

I
Am
Abundant

Believe that there is abundance in everything.
Trust that there is enough for everyone, even you.
Abundance is always trying to flow to you, let it in.
When you feel abundant, you allow it to come to you.
Know that there is more than enough of everything you want.
Let go of the fear that you cannot have something someone else has.
Release feelings of lack and begin to believe that your life is full of abundance.

I am abundant because

....

....

....

I am abundant because

....

....

....

I am abundant because

....

....

....

I
Am
Where I Am Meant to Be

Wherever you are in life.
Whatever is going on right now.
Know that you are in the right place.
Even if it doesn't seem like it right now.
Even if you're going through a tough time.
Everything happening to you, is happening for you.
Everything will work out; you are where you're meant to be.

I am where I am meant to be because

....

....

....

I am where I am meant to be because

....

....

....

I am where I am meant to be because

....

....

....

I
Am
On the Right Path

Everything you are doing is taking you to where you want to go.
If you need to change direction, your intuition will tell you.
The universe is always guiding you towards joy.
You are going in the right direction.
You are on the right path.

I am on the right path because

....
....
....

I am on the right path because

....
....
....

I am on the right path because

....
....
....

I
Am
A Magnet

You are a magnet for love.
You are a magnet for good luck.
You are a magnet for health and prosperity.
You are a magnet for wealth and abundance.
Everything you want is gravitating towards you.
Feel everything you want being pulled towards you.

I am a magnet because

....

....

....

I am a magnet because

....

....

....

I am a magnet because

....

....

....

I
Am
the Master of
My Thoughts

You are the master of your thoughts.
Let your thoughts attract good to you.
Change thoughts that no longer serve you.
Choose thoughts that make you feel good today.

I am the master of my thoughts because

....
....
....

I am the master of my thoughts because

....
....
....

I am the master of my thoughts because

....
....
....

I
Am
Always in the Right Place at the Right Time

Everything you want is flowing to you.
Everything that happens is happening for you.
Everywhere you go and everything you do is right for you.
You are being guided to have everything when you are meant to.
You are always in the right place at the right time to receive what you want.

I am in the right place at the right time because

....
....
....

I am in the right place at the right time because

....
....
....

I am in the right place at the right time because

....
....
....

I
Am
Always Manifesting

The law of attraction is always working.
Your thoughts are always manifesting.
Feel good to manifest good to you.
You do not have to try to manifest.
You are already manifesting.

I am always manifesting because

....
....
....

I am always manifesting because

....
....
....

I am always manifesting because

....
....
....

I
Am
Magical

Believe in magic and magical things will happen.
You deserve some magic in your life.
Whatever you expect, you get.
The magic is within you.
You just have to see it.

I am magical because

....
....
....

I am magical because

....
....
....

I am magical because

....
....
....

I
Am
A Diamond

You
are unique.
Show your sparkle.
You are strong and elite.
You are beautiful and brilliant.
Like diamonds, you may take time to form.
But either way, you are a diamond.
Get ready to shine bright.
Light up the
world.

I am a diamond because

I am a diamond because

I am a diamond because

I
Am
A Phoenix

When you feel defeated and lost.
Let your tears revive and awaken you.
Let your pain be the fire that burns away the old you.
Let yourself rise from the ashes like a Phoenix.
Be reborn into a new version of you.
There is a Phoenix in all of us.
You are a Phoenix.

I am a Phoenix because

....
....
....

I am a Phoenix because

....
....
....

I am a Phoenix because

....
....
....

I
Am
In Alignment

Raise your vibration and start to feel good; come into alignment with what you want.
Choose to feel good even though your manifestations haven't arrived yet.
Believe that everything is working out the way you want it to.
Trust that the universe will bring you the highest good.
YOU ARE IN ALIGNMENT.

I am in alignment because

....

....

....

I am in alignment because

....

....

....

I am in alignment because

....

....

....

Printed in Great Britain
by Amazon

18770595R00066